How to Recover from Loss

Understanding and Recovering from Grief

Robyn Ledwith Mar

The Lord is close to the broken hearted
and saves those who are crushed in spirit. Psalm 34:18

Cover photograph by Robyn Ledwith Mar

ISBN-13: 978-1479134793
ISBN-10: 1479134791

HOW TO RECOVER FROM LOSS

Contents

HOW TO RECOVER FROM LOSS

Contents

HOW TO RECOVER FROM LOSS

Introduction

This book is about loss. If you have been in a support group for grief or loss, you would have found that everyone views their loss differently. There is a tendency to feel that my loss is greater than your loss. But it is important not to make judgments about the severity of anyone else's loss or pain. Whether it is a crib death, a teenage suicide, or the loss of a spouse, we cannot judge who has suffered more. We have all suffered the loss of someone sometime in our lives; we have all experienced our own pain in our own way. In this book I am going to talk about the grieving experience in general, about the many types of loss, and about how to begin the recovery process. No matter what the loss, this book is about choosing to recover, how to recover, and about hope.

From the time I wrote the first books on grieving, which developed out of a grief recovery class for widows and widowers, I have become more aware of how we need to learn to cope with grief in other areas of life. It is not only the death of a loved one or a friend that can cause pain and anger. Receiving a medical report that says you have a long term, life threatening, or terminal physical condition or disease is almost as great a loss for us individually as the death of a loved one. If we are ill, we have lost our sense of well-being. We may be facing years of disability and dependency. As we view our new circumstances, we, too can go through a time of grieving. If it is a loved one who is ill, we are sometimes at a loss as to how to respond.

Because of my own experience with cancer and other health issues, I have been confronted by my own loss of health. Additionally, mortality has become more of a reality than a concept. I have seen friends become ill with life threatening or terminal illnesses and watched their struggle with anxiety and faith. The necessity of being able to deal with that on-going grief, theirs as well as mine, has become as important as accepting the death of someone close to me.

I lost my husband to cancer when I was 56 years old. That loss was followed by the deaths of my parents, and then, later, close friends. It seemed like each loss intensified the previous pain of losing someone I loved. I was fortunate in being able to lead classes in grief recovery and, at the same time, work through my own remembered pain. It is out of that experience that I have written this book.

Recovery does not mean forgetting our loss; we can never do that. But recovery does mean remembering your loss without the paralyzing pain. It means being able to move on in your life and not being stuck in grief forever. It means facing and working through your grief and getting your life started again. You will never forget what has happened to you, but you can recover.

Robyn Ledwith Mar

HOW TO RECOVER FROM LOSS

"Blessed are those who mourn, for they will be comforted."
Matthew 5: 4

Chapter 1. Understanding Loss and Grief

"The last time I saw Bob, he was going out the door to work. I was busy with the children and didn't take the time to give him a kiss goodbye. He tried to call me during the day, but I never got back to him. I never dreamed that I would never see him again. I'll never forget the call from the police, telling me that he had collapsed on the way home. I just can't believe that he's gone. I never had the chance to tell him goodbye."

"We knew that Marian's cancer was spreading and that there wasn't too much hope. Yet we continued to pray and plan for a future. I was so certain that God would heal her. Why did he let her die? I can't stop thinking about it."

"My Dad had such a long illness that we were able to prepare for his death. He had planned everything and he seemed to be at peace. I thought that I was ready to let him go. I had no idea that it would be so hard. I miss him so much. I'll never get over it."

"I couldn't believe the diagnosis that Jimmy was going to die. He was only 8 years old! Those six months that he was so sick are still just a blur to me. I can't seem to stop crying. I can't do the simplest things. I don't think that I'll ever recover."

"When the doctor told me that I had cancer, I didn't believe it. I couldn't believe that they were going to remove my breast. But they did, and I don't think that I will ever be the same. Every time I look at myself I can't help crying. I'd rather be dead."

"Nothing can be so bad as to have someone commit suicide. My son was only 18 years old. Why didn't he talk to us? What was his reason? It's not as though it was an accident; he made the decision. I feel so guilty. It must have been my fault."

Loss: the universal experience

Loss is the one emotional experience common to all people. We are all born, we grow, we love, and we lose loved ones. Eventually we die, a thought that is pushed out of our minds until we are forced to face our mortality. Unless we die prematurely, we will all see our parents die, some of us will lose brothers and sisters, uncles and aunts, and friends. If we are extremely unfortunate, we might lose a child to illness, accident, or suicide. And, if we marry, unless we suffer common disaster, one partner of each married couple will lose his or her spouse; we will either precede our spouse in death, or we will survive to be a widow or widower. If we are married, we all have a 50% chance of being a widow or widower. Unless we have no relatives, friends, or live in an isolated cave separated from humanity, we all have a 100% chance of experiencing a personal loss in our lives.

As humans, we cannot avoid death and loss. Death is inevitable. Our birth and our dying bracket our lives. We do not die because God is angry with us or wishes to punish us. We die because we are human and because it is part of our natural life.

In our lives we will experience many kinds of loss, some life changing, others less damaging to our lives. We may process each loss differently, but our reactions are surprisingly universal, and the steps through our grieving are very similar.

The losses that we may encounter in life are varied:

> The small losses: car keys, earrings, and other things that can upset us
> The loss of a job or income
> The loss of health, either short, long term, or terminal: such as cancer or dementia
> The loss of a home through moving, fire, or vandalism
> Losses that can loom large in our lives such as losing a pet or valuable belongings
> Estrangements or divorce, as painful and emotionally draining as a death
> And finally, the death of loved ones and, ultimately, the prospect of our own death

The pattern of personal loss

When someone has lost a loved one, the circumstances surrounding that death follow a well-worn path. The general pattern is usually as follows:

1. The events before the loss: sickness, depression. If there has been a long illness, such as cancer, ALS, Parkinson's, or Alzheimer's disease, the survivor may be physically and/or emotionally worn out from caregiving.

2. The loss, which is a death or loss of our health. The shock of death is acute, even if the person has been ill a long time. If there has been an accident, there is even greater shock and continuing disbelief that this could have happened.

3. The initial reaction to the loss: extreme feelings of sadness and loss, including the physical symptoms of grief.

4. Disorganization: often the survivors feel intense despair and hopelessness. They frequently cannot cope with life.

5. Slow reorganization: working through the stages of grief, regaining hope.

6. Recovery

A description of grief

Grief is the emotional state that accompanies any loss. It is the process of understanding and adjusting to the changes in our lives. It is almost always painful. Loss can be overwhelming in its immensity or can be as brief and momentary as lost car keys. As we will see, the process of grieving will be the same, whether it lasts for a year or for a moment. We all go through the same reactions and steps, and understanding them can make it easier.

Even knowing this, we are surprised when faced with the loss of friends, relatives, or close family members. Our first reaction is disbelief, a sense of unreality. How could this have happened? If the death has been unexpected or happens away from home, we may have great trouble believing that it has occurred. We may expect our loved one to walk back into the house, to hear their voice again, or even to hear that the news was not true. That is why it is important that we go through the rituals of acknowledging death. We go to funerals or we go to ceremonies of various faiths. We need to see the deceased, maybe have a quiet time to sit with them, and be surrounded by friends who can help us accept this difficult to believe event.

When we experience loss, or when we encounter grief, we need to understand what is going on. Grief is not a mysterious occurrence, it is not abnormal, and it is not something that we should fear. Grief is a process that we must go through to recover our equilibrium and go on with life. God never intended that we stay stuck in grief. He urges us to cross that dark valley and go to the other side because he will go with us. He has a plan for our lives, and we cannot fulfill that plan if we are forever sunk in our grief.

How can we learn to better understand our grief as well as that of others? If we do not understand what happens when we grieve, or the stages of grief, or the recovery process, we cannot understand our feelings or understand how to deal with them.

When we are grieving, how can we learn to accept our grief and acknowledge our feelings? First, we need to understand our emotions and be honest with ourselves about how we feel.

We must:

Learn to express, not to repress, our feelings
> Accept that our loss cannot be replaced
> Accept other people's help in grieving
> Understand that it will take time to recover
> Try not to have regrets about the past; we did the best we could

How to help yourself:

> Ask for practical help from friends and relatives
> Don't be hard on yourself; don't expect too much
> Allow yourself to mourn; you don't have to be brave

Find responsive friends who can listen to you
Let others express their grief to you
Be honest about your grieving
Don't worry that you are "burdening" your friends

Throughout this book you will be learning more about the grieving process, how to face your loss, and the nature of grief. You will also learn about choosing to recover. But now, during the initial stages of loss, immediately following the event and even months after, it is also important that you take care of yourself, both physically and emotionally.

Your decision: To recognize that you have suffered loss, are in deep grief, and need help.

Questions:

1. On a separate sheet of paper, describe as fully as you can the circumstances of your loss. (This may be the start of journaling, or writing down your feelings. Many people find it extremely helpful during the recovery process. There are pages at the end of the book where you can write.)

2. Describe your physical reactions at the time of loss

3. What are some things that you can do now to take better care of yourself?

Personal prayer:
Tell God about your pain and how much you hurt. Ask for his comforting arms to support you. Our God understands grief. Jesus wept when he saw how Mary and Martha were grieving the death of their brother Lazarus. (John 11:17-44)

HOW TO RECOVER FROM LOSS

Even though I walk through the valley of the shadow of death, I will fear no evil;
for you are with me; your rod and your staff, they comfort me. Psalm 23: 4

Chapter 2. Reaction to Loss

The numbness and shock
When this has happened to you, when you look back on the event, you can recognize that after your loss you were in a state of shock. Whether the death has been anticipated or is unexpected, you find that you are disoriented, frightened and confused. You can't grasp what has happened. Your world has stopped. There seems to be no future, only blackness and emptiness.

Each of the stories in the former chapter represents a specific type of loss, and each is unique. However, when we talk about bereavement of any kind, we realize that the experience is universal. The circumstances and the timing of the death may vary, but the process of moving through grief is similar and has recognizable stages.

How you feel when you grieve
During this first state of shock, which may last for weeks, you may feel numb, even though underneath there is terrible pain. You know that you must get through the first few days or weeks of your loss, so you refuse to feel the pain. You may be so turned inward that you are unaware of what you are doing. You may be trying so hard to control your emotions that you deny yourself the comfort of tears. It is important that you give yourself permission to feel the loss, to grieve, to cry.

While you are grieving you may not be able to pay attention to everyday matters. It may seem that you are out of touch with reality. Actually, your mind is in a state of emergency, similar to the body's reaction to a major wound. You may not hear what others say to you or respond coherently. You may initially be able to cope and seem efficient, only to collapse a few days later.

There are certain physical reactions to extreme grief. It is helpful to understand them so that you don't mistake them for signs of craziness. They are not permanent, and are generally shared by all those who experience loss.

Some common reactions during the first weeks of loss are:

1. Disbelief and a sense of unreality. You can't believe what has happened.
2. Sudden or constant crying and sobbing
3. Feeling numb, confused, or disoriented
4. Sleeplessness or unusual sleep patterns
5. Physical pain or illness
6. Periods of extreme anxiety

7. A sense of isolation
8. Becoming hyperactively busy or being unable to concentrate at work
9. Momentarily forgetting that the loss has occurred
10. Being overwhelmed by memories
11. Fear of the future: how can I survive with this loss?

How others view you

Other people don't know how to deal with loss either. They are embarrassed by your grief. Often they don't know what to say or they try to encourage you to act as though you have already recovered. They want their help to be effective, but don't always know how to be helpful: they are afraid of your emotions, as it is threatening to them.

They don't want to talk about it: death and loss are uncomfortable subjects
They want you to be brave: your emotions are difficult for them to handle
They expect you to recover quickly: "You really should be feeling better by now."
They think that if you keep busy it will help you recover

Our society doesn't want to look at death or loss. We are taught as children that we are to repress our feelings, replace our losses, grieve alone, let time alone heal our wounds, live with our regrets, and never trust to love again.

But we can express our feelings without embarrassment
We can accept our losses and not seek replacements but look forward
We can grieve in community, with friends and those who are close to us
We can seek help from God if we are believers
We can reconcile ourselves to what we regret and forgive ourselves
We can learn to trust again

Pretending you are OK

Sometimes those who are grieving are so successful at convincing others that they are OK that they appear to achieve an amazing recovery. You want the approval of others, so you put a smile on your face and pretend that everything is OK. The effort involved in stuffing your emotions and pretending that you are doing better than you are is not good for you and can lead to behavioral disorders such as over-medication or alcohol abuse. It is important that those who are grieving not put on a good show to please others or meet their expectations about recovery. You are a unique individual and should deal with grief at your own pace and in your own way. You don't have to prove that you are brave.

If you listen to God's word, you will learn that God tells us to accept and acknowledge our feelings of grief. All through the Old Testament, God's people are told to mourn and weep for their dead. Jesus wept for Lazarus. We are not told to bury our feelings and deny our grief. We are told to weep. It is important that you cry; tears will cleanse your heart so that God can start to heal you.

When the grief returns: but I thought I was doing so well....
When the first shock and numbness have passed there is a time when you are running on pure energy. You take care of practical matters: lawyers, business matters, and immediate problems. You have been doing well, thinking, "This isn't so bad." But then, when the initial crisis has passed and you think that you may be returning to normal, the full realization of what has happened hits you. You see an empty future stretching before you; life has become futile and meaningless. Nothing seems to matter.

"I thought I was doing so well. Everyone said that I was getting back to normal, whatever that is! I don't understand how depressed I have become. It's like I've gone back to the beginning. Will it ever get better?"

As this second wave of grief occurs, you may experience some new feelings and emotions. A new realization of the extent of your loss may overwhelm you. It is as though when the first shock wears off you are now able to feel the full impact of reality. This is not a dream. You cannot go back. You may suddenly perceive that:

> You are no longer sure who you are; you have lost your sense of identity
> Your life has irrevocably changed and will continue to change
> You've lost your ability to cope with ordinary things
> You are trying to be super busy and it's not working
> Your family relationships have become strained
> You are still angry about the loss
> You are increasingly depressed
> You are impatient with others and the world at large
> You may have slipped into destructive behavior with alcohol or drugs

How you can help yourself:
It is important to understand that you are grieving for much more than your spouse, parent, child, relative, friend, or health. You have lost much of your life and how you are used to living. You are grieving for yourself and beginning to understand that you will have to build a new world and a new life.

You need to recognize what you can do to make yourself feel better:

> Slow down: mourning is hard work and requires a lot of energy
> Eat sensibly and moderately
> Take as much time off from responsibilities as possible
> Maintain healthy living habits: physical exercise, get enough rest, relax
> Give yourself permission to cry, to grieve, to feel bad
> Express your emotions at appropriate times without embarrassment
> Seek the companionship of those who love you, to talk and to listen
> Get professional help if you need it

What do you need to do? You must:

Make the decision to work through the suffering and grief to recovery
Choose to fight rather than to take flight
Deal with circumstances rather than denying them
Start to make changes in your life.
Abide in your faith and trust God
Know that God is in control of all things, even if it seems unlikely

Your decision: To begin to understand where you are in the grieving process.

Questions:

1. Have you experienced a second wave of grief? When? How did you feel?

2. Have you been putting on a good act, pretending that you are OK when you really don't feel that you are OK?

3. What are some of the things you personally could do to feel better?

Personal prayer:
If you are in the midst of this second wave of grief, tell God about the darkness of your life and ask him to bring light and comfort to you.

HOW TO RECOVER FROM LOSS

Turn to me and be gracious to me, for I am lonely and afflicted.
The troubles of my heart have multiplied; free me from my anguish.
Look upon my affliction and my distress and take away all my sins. Psalm 25: 16-18

Chapter 3. The Grieving Process

If you are faced with your own or another's grief, it is helpful to understand what is going to happen. Loss and grieving is a process. There are recognizable stages that one goes through, although not everyone goes through them in the same order or according to the same timetable.

There is no correct way to grieve. Although there are recognized stages to our grieving, not everyone goes through them in the same order. It is a fluid process with much overlapping of feelings and emotions. The grieving process is the God-given gift of slowly allowing ourselves to accept what has happened.

Elisabeth Kübler-Ross was a pioneer in the study of grief. Although her work was primarily with the dying, the stages of grieving which she identified can also be applied to those who have suffered the loss. She writes that the dying person passes through five stages of coping with death. The first is that of denial and isolation, the second is anger, the third is bargaining, the fourth is depression, and the final stage is that of acceptance. Perhaps those of us who have been with a spouse, relative, or friend through a lengthy illness have been able to observe these stages, and perhaps have witnessed the acceptance and peace of the final stage.

Stages of grief
The stages of grief can apply as well to those who have suffered loss as to those who are dying. It is important to understand these stages when dealing with anyone who is ill or bereaved. Not everyone goes through these stages in the same order. It is a fluid process with much over-lapping of feelings and emotions.

1. Denial and isolation

> The initial reaction to death or threatening medical news can be denial: "I don't believe this is happening!" It may be days before the news really sinks in, before you can face their illness or the finality of death. You may not be able to face your own grief. You may deny your pain, appear to be emotionally strong, and more interested in being a support for others. Sometimes the reaction to a suicide is one of denial: the death is accepted, but the circumstances are not.

> Denial is often listed as a stage of grief as the reality may be too hard to bear and you may not want to believe that your loved one is dead or that your health is threatened. It may be days before the news really sinks in, before you can face

your own grief by denying your pain, appearing to be strong, and being more of a support for others than taking care of yourself.

2. Anger

Anger may be harder to recognize and difficult to respond to. Many people who are grieving deny that they feel anger. If there is a death, anger can be directed against doctors, hospitals, or anyone perceived to be at fault for the death. Sometimes people turn their anger against themselves for things not done or actions not taken. It is important to remember that feeling anger is normal, but care should taken that it is not harmful to yourself or others.

There are often feelings of abandonment, or resentment if domestic or financial matters have not been settled. Frequently the survivor may express anger that the loved one died sooner than had been expected: "Why did he leave me alone? Now what am I going to do?" "How am I to go on living without her?" This type of anger is common and needs to be worked through before you can move on. It may even be necessary to forgive your loved ones for having died.

3. Bargaining

Sometimes people feel that they must bargain with God. They often promise God many things if only he will spare their health or the one they love. It is not that God does not hear our prayers; it is that he is sovereign and rules our lives according to his plan. Why he allows illness and death to come is often beyond our understanding, but it is necessary to remember that eventually we all will die. It is the manner and timing of illness or death that may be hard to accept.

4. Depression

Depression is another stage of grieving; one that is only too familiar to grievers. These are truly the feelings of staggering through the valley of the shadow of death. It is not unusual for a bereaved person to suffer physical illness from grief. Those who are ill or grieving may stumble and feel that they are not able to get up again. They may barely be able to get through the day and lie awake through the night. It is very much a physical state and can be dangerous. The depression may lift for a while, but return later. Depression may require professional help if it continues.

5. Acceptance

And finally, the peace of acceptance. Accepting loss as part of life. If there is a death, being able to rejoice in the memories of a full and complete life together, or recognizing that although the loved one is gone, there is still a life to live. The sadness will always be there, but the stabbing pain is gone. This is emotional recovery. Not forgetting those who have died, but letting them live on in our memories. If there is illness, it means being able to accept the circumstances and being reconciled to them.

You may feel that you have not experienced all these stages in grieving the death of your loved one or loss of health. For example, many people do not experience anger at the loved one, but still may be angry with some of the circumstances of the death. You are not abnormal if you have not experienced all of these stages, but whether or not you think they apply to you, it is helpful to be aware of them and to understand them.

These stages can apply to anyone who has had a loss. Recovering from loss is a process; it is not a permanent state. However, when you are first flattened with grief, it is hard to imagine that you will ever get better. You may feel that you are in a deep dark pit with no escape. What is important is that you must have the hope that recovery is possible. There is a ladder that will enable you to climb out of that pit. That is the certain hope that you can recover. The first step is to understand your grieving process. The second is that you choose to recover. It is very important to understand that only you have the power to make that choice happen. You are not powerless in your grief, although you may feel powerless in the grip of your despair.

If we do not enter into the grieving process after the death of a loved one, we will be denied the healing. We will live half-lives, not letting go of the past and not entering fully into the future. It takes time and work. For the bereaved, it may be as long as two years before we are fully healed, but it is worth it. We owe it to those who have shared our lives to climb up out of our dark valley and restart the journey toward a new life.

The Question: Why?

When speaking of anger, there is sometimes anger with God for allowing the death or illness. This can be a difficult question for a believer: "Why did God let this happen if God is good?" And that, of course, is hard, even for a theologian, to answer. I have given up trying to understand why illness, accident, or death comes when and how it does. We know that we become ill and die because we are human. But I believe that God does not make mistakes. God has reasons that we do not know. He says in Isaiah 55: 8-9: *"For my thoughts are not your thoughts, neither are your ways my ways," declares the Lord. "As the heavens are higher than the earth, so are my ways higher than your ways and my thoughts than your thoughts."*

God has his own plan for each of our lives. God says in Jeremiah 29:11: *"For I know the plans I have for you," declares the Lord, "plans to prosper you and not to harm you, plans to give you a hope and a future."* But although we may know this in our heads, in our hearts we are always ambushed by grief. Even if the death is expected, the event is still a shock. Whether it is a husband who never returns from the office, a wife who does not survive her cancer, a teenager killed in an accident, or a suicide in the family, it is always a shock.

What I believe is that in the center of life is sorrow and loss, and it is there that you can find God. He is a God of sorrow: he knows that all life incurs loss and in your sorrow and loss you can move closer to God.

But God is also a God of joy. He says, "Be comforted! I am with you always." He will heal you and bring you joy. He will bring you a hope and a future. And finally there will no longer be sorrow nor loss when you and your loved ones are with the Lord. He has given us his promise.

What if you are angry with God? Your faith may be shaken at this time. You may feel that God has not answered your prayers in allowing your loved one to die, or allowing him or her to become ill. Anger at God can be a normal response to the death of a loved one. Your friends and relatives may be concerned if you question your faith, but you need to work through your anger with God and not feel judged for it. Sometimes people give up on their faith because they weren't able to resolve their feelings of anger. If this happens the one who is grieving is cut off from the most powerful support resource he or she has, which is the power of prayer. Prayer can comfort your heart and ease your mind.

What can you do if you are angry with God? First, you can boldly go to God and tell him that you are angry without feeling guilty about it. Ask for his help as you search the Scriptures for his promises to us and look for the examples he has given us in the Bible. Many people in the Bible were angry with God, but he answered them, even though the answers weren't always easy. And then continue to pray about it. Ask God to help you through the grieving process, knowing that you can count on his unfailing love to help you overcome your grief.

Your decision: Will you trust God to help you move on through your grief to recovery?

Questions:

1. Can you recognize the stages of grieving in your own experience? Describe them.

2. Is understanding more about the grieving process helpful to you? In what way?

3. Do you believe that God meets you within your sorrow and loss? Have you had this experience?

4. Are you angry with God? If so, write a letter to God expressing your anger and how you feel about your loss. Be specific about why you are angry.

Personal prayer:
Ask God to help you understand why he has allowed this sorrow to come into your life. Let him comfort you with his love.

HOW TO RECOVER FROM LOSS

The Lord is close to the broken hearted
and saves those who are crushed in spirit. Psalm 34:18

Chapter 4. Facing Your Loss

Why are we surprised and frightened by grief?
Death, illness, and loss are a part of life, so why are we so surprised and afraid when we are confronted with grief? We are surprised by grief because we somehow think that tragedy and sadness can't touch us.

Grief frightens us because:
"It could happen to me." Loss is a reminder of our own mortality
We feel helpless in the face of tragedy
We don't know what to say and are afraid that we will say the wrong thing
We might get pulled into someone else's grief
We don't know if they'll get better and we may have to be in a caretaking role
We are afraid of our emotion: it is threatening
We don't want to talk about it: death and illness are uncomfortable subjects
We want others to be brave: emotions are difficult for us to handle
We hope we will recover quickly, whether from a loss or illness

Why don't we know how to deal with grief?
In the midst of grief the bereaved may have difficulty in knowing how to cope. They may be so torn by their emotions that they can't find a solid foundation for their feet. They reach back into their past and may find little or no experience to help them with the present grief. Relatives and friends may not know what to say; at times their attempts to comfort are not helpful. Why don't we know how to deal with loss?

Some of us were fortunate and grew up in loving and expressive families where the deaths of our relatives and friends were accepted and mourned. But many of us were conditioned as children not to express our grief. As children we might have learned that we must deny our feelings or that it was somehow improper to show grief. How many times were we told not to cry, not to bother someone who was grieving, or were sent away from the grieving adults?

As children we did not learn how to grieve:
We were conditioned not to show grief
We learned to hide our feelings
We did not always witness adults grieving

As adults:
We are embarrassed by grief: both our own and others' grief
We don't want to be involved with grief

It's not only us, but other people don't know how to deal with loss either. They are embarrassed by our grief. Often they don't know what to say or they try to encourage us to act as though we have already recovered. They want their help to be effective, but don't always know how to be helpful. We, also, may not know how to speak or act. To understand another person's grief, we must first understand our own.

As an adult you may now be faced with an overwhelming loss. How can you learn to accept your grief and acknowledge your feelings? You must try to understand your emotions and be honest with yourself about how you feel. As a grieving adult you must learn to express your feelings and you must learn to accept other people's help in grieving, no matter how bumbling or inappropriate.

> Learn to express, not to repress, your feelings
> Accept that your loss cannot be replaced
> Accept others' help in grieving
> Understand that it will take time to recover
> Try not to have regrets about the past; accept that you did the best you could

Why don't we know what to say?
It is impossible to know another person's feelings. No one will ever know how you feel or the depth of your pain. Yet, we all try to comfort those who are in pain. The only true response is, "I'm sorry."

People may speak in platitudes that are not helpful.

> "If you just get busy it will be easier"
> "You must forget the past and move on"
> "Your loss was for the best; your loved one is with God"

People may make well meant but inappropriate remarks:

> After the funeral of your spouse: "Have you thought about remarriage?"
> A week after your husband or wife has died: "Why don't you try to meet someone and start dating?"
> Perhaps your mother just died: "You are fortunate that she didn't have to suffer long."
> Your father has just died: "He had a long life, it was time for him to go."
> You just lost one of your children: "You still have your other children."

These comments may have good intentions, but they aren't helpful to you now. Remember to be kind to people who want to help you. They don't realize that what they are saying could be hurtful to you. No matter how reasonable their comments seems to them, you have lost a loved one and it will take time to recover.

I still recall standing at the door of my home throughout the long afternoon reception for friends who had come to my husband's graveside memorial. It seemed that all I did was to murmur comforting things to the visitors. They all wanted to share their grief with me. So often we must put aside our pain and try to understand the pain and awkwardness of others as they attempt to say the right thing.

Your decision: To let yourself be honest about your feelings

Questions:

1. What did you learn as a child regarding reaction to loss? How well did your family cope with death?

2. Do you feel that other people don't understand your grief? How can you better express your feelings to them?

3. List some of the inappropriate remarks people have made to you. How did you respond? Can you remember thoughtless remarks you might have made in the past?

Personal Prayer:
If you are angry, tell God about your anger and how unfair life can be. Ask him to help you deal with your anger in a constructive way.

HOW TO RECOVER FROM LOSS

"And surely, I am with you always, to the end of the age." Matthew 28: 20. "As I was with Moses, so I will be with you; I will never leave you nor forsake you." Joshua 1: 5

Chapter 5. Specific Kinds of Loss

There are many kinds of loss described here, but in the heart of each mourner, his or her loss is like no other loss. Although the general pattern for grieving loss is the same, there will still be differences in how you grieve. If there has been a death, the closeness of your relationship to the deceased has a great deal to do with your experience and how long it will take you to recover. If you have suffered a personal physical loss, such as your health, that will be different, too. Therefore, we will look at the specific kinds of loss and how people may react to those losses.

Spouse

If you are married, you have a very good chance of losing your spouse to death or illness. When we marry, we believe that we will be together forever. If your spouse dies, the loss can be catastrophic. Divorce can also be catastrophic, but it is different and has its own pain. The person whose spouse dies often feels as though they have been cut in two and that the wound will never heal. These are some of the specific issues facing a new widow or widower:

> The loss of your life partner, best friend, and supporter
> The loss of your defined role as a wife or husband
> Unexpected estate and financial problems
> A possible financial loss and a major change in your life style
> Loneliness: waking up to an empty house
> Depression: not being able to get out of bed or care for yourself
> An inability to see how you will be able to live in the future

If there has been a long illness, and you were the caregiver, this role, too, is gone, often leaving a deep sense of loss of meaning for your life. This is especially true if your spouse had suffered from Alzheimer's disease or a stroke that extended the caregiving period by years.

It is important for you to talk about your loss. You need to be heard, but the world seems to go on without your spouse and seemingly doesn't care. The greatest problems for the widow or widower are the indifference of the world and loneliness. Your friends can help you by:

> Not expecting a quick recovery
> Having a willingness to listen
> Not avoiding you socially
> Helping you find a recovery group

Becoming part of a grief recovery group is especially beneficial. There you can meet others with the same experience and can learn about the stages and effects of grieving. Also, you can find new friends to help you recover and start your new life.

Parents

Although the death of a parent would seem to be in the natural order of things, the fact of death doesn't seem to be real. You never really thought it would happen. Even if there has been illness or the death is expected, the actual event can be intensely painful. When you lose a parent, you lose someone with whom you have had heavy emotional ties. If you have lost both your dad and your mom, that makes you an orphan. It also means that you have moved up a notch on the mortality scale: you are next in line. That alone is enough to make you feel vulnerable and uneasy.

The loss of a parent is also often accompanied by the distressing burdens of either taking the responsibility for the surviving parent, or settling the estate. Simply disposing of household or personal belongings can be extremely time consuming and stressful.

All of these emotions–grief, feelings of abandonment, vulnerability, possible regrets–can result in many of the same emotional and physical patterns as that of losing a spouse. It does not help to be reminded that your parent had a long life and that death should be expected. Depending upon the relationship, this loss can be just as devastating as any other. Often, the grief of the surviving parent is so isolating that both young and adult children may feel estranged; they may feel that they have lost both parents: one to death, the other to grief.

Children

Losing a child is every parent's worst nightmare. I cannot think of anything that could be said to comfort a grieving parent. Their child is gone; their child's voice is silenced forever. The child does not have to be young; losing a child of any age is traumatic. They are part of us. It is not in the natural order of things; we never want to outlive our children. If you are a believer, knowing that your child is now with the Lord may help to comfort you, but it does not lift your grief.

The circumstances of loss of a small child are usually illness, possibly infant crib death, or accidents. A teenager may die in an auto accident, or as a result of alcohol or drug related abuses, or sadly, as a suicide. Children in their 20's and 30's are also vulnerable, and adult children also die from accidents and illness.

The death of a child of any age in a family can cause serious emotional upheaval. Often the reaction is denial and silence because the grief is too hard to bear. If there has been a long illness, in all probability the parents were so involved in trying to save the child that they had no time to mourn. Therefore the most difficult part will be the day-to-day realization that their child is gone. It will take a long time for the parents and family to regain their balance.

It is very important for the family to grieve together, sharing their grief, and working toward recovery. Especially if the deceased is a teenager or adult, the surviving children may often need professional counseling or a support group to help keep the lines of communication open. It is also helpful for the parents to find a support group, such as Compassionate Friends, a national organization that offers grief support after the death of a child.

If it is an older child, especially if there has been a suicide, the family may draw into isolation. Any loss of a child is so great and is so threatening to society that few people are willing to be close to the bereaved. The grieving parents need to talk about their child and their loss and to resolve issues of blame. They need time and space in which to grieve. They may never completely recover and often the parents' marriage does not survive the loss. It is important that they not be stigmatized for the severity of their loss; they will need a lot of support, both from friends and professionals.

Brothers and Sisters

When young children lose a brother or sister they must cope with the mystery of the finality of death. Hopefully, there will be a caring adult to help the children walk through this emotional minefield. There are many books designed to help a child try to understand what has happened; there are also professional support groups that provide support for bereaved children. Some of the problems that may arise in reaction to this loss are poor health, emotional instability, "acting out" in rebellion against the loss, and poor response at school.

For the adult child who has lost a sibling, there can be many conflicting emotions. Regret, guilt, anger, and a sense of inappropriateness may be present. The surviving child of any age may feel that they should have died rather than their brother or sister. The fabric of the family may be seriously strained as the parents suffer in their grief. Instead of turning to each other and the family for comfort, many parents become distant and turned inward. Not talking about the death will cause alienation; it is difficult for a family to heal unless they can reach out to one another in love.

Relatives and Friends

Our families are made up of parents, grandparents, brothers, sisters, aunts, uncles, cousins, and often friends that are part of the family. The death of any one of these can cause great pain for the whole family. Sometimes the family doesn't handle the loss well and communications break down, splintering the family into isolated units. It is important that the family grieve together, not being afraid to show their tears and being able to express their grief to one another. Everyone feels the consequences of the loss a little differently, but the suffering can still be very great for all. If a family can share their grief openly and talk about their loss, they will recover more rapidly. Unresolved grief in a family can persist for years, damaging the relationships through regrets, guilt, or blaming.

Sometime families resist counseling, but recovery is more likely if they get help and choose to recover. As a comforting friend, you may be able to help them make that choice.

When a friend dies, whether through accident, illness, or suicide, you can suffer as much as if it were a family member. Depending upon the closeness of the friend, you may be as affected as if you had lost a relative. You will have the same reactions and go through many of the same stages. We are all shocked when we hear of the death of even an acquaintance and we need to process and absorb that news. Gathering together with your friends and attending a memorial service can be helpful.

We all need to take the loss of friends seriously and be understanding of grief. Among older people, the loss of friends signals the approach of the end of life; they have fewer people close to them. Young adults can be extremely sensitive to the death of a brother, sister, or peer, yet they may have a difficult time expressing it. Teenagers can be thrown into serious depression if a friend dies, especially if it is a violent death. It is important that we be aware of their suffering, letting them know that we care, and perhaps finding help for them through group counseling at their school or church.

Suicide

Death by suicide, whether of parent, sibling, spouse, or child, presents a very difficult situation. Suicide is different because:

1. Someone whom you love or have deeply cared about has chosen to leave you, not by abandonment or divorce, but by premeditated death
2. The deceased has renounced all possibility of help from you
3. It's like an argument where they have the last word
4. There is no opportunity to say goodbye

Over half of the survivors (those who have lost someone to suicide) are depressed or have psychological or physical problems that seem to be related to their role as survivor.

What happens to the survivor after someone commits suicide:

1. Feelings or guilt or shame may be the overriding emotions
2. Friends may avoid you
3. Friends and relatives may act as though you are responsible
4. Suicide may seem to be an accusation that your love wasn't enough
5. You may feel that you are carrying a sign that proclaims: "My child (husband, wife) committed suicide."

Suicide is an unnatural act and the family of the person who kills himself may be subjected to public dismay and criticism. There are still clergy who view the death of a person by suicide as a sinful act, although there is no scriptural basis for such an opinion.

There is often the unreal expectation from society that life will go on as usual, which it won't. A suicide can be more painful for the family than other kinds of death and much harder to acknowledge. The survivors often suffer from guilt and shame that prevent normal mourning and the silence that surrounds suicide gets in the way of the healing that comes with normal mourning.

Most survivors become overwhelmed by anger, despair, depression, and guilt, but others are able to work their way through the tragedy. It is important for all survivors to understand what they are going through, to recognize the emotions that are part of grieving after suicide, and to recognize when they are stuck in those emotions and cannot move on. Survivors may have thoughts of suicide themselves. In this case, there should be professional help or intervention.

Loss of Health

The loss of our health can throw us into a panic. We may be faced with the possibility of a long debilitating illness possibly resulting in our own death. We were healthy, now we are not. We are losing something very important and it is a major loss. Our life is changing and we mourn that change. This, in effect, is not much different than the emotions we feel when we are bereaved, and we can experience the same stages of grief as someone who is bereaved. In fact, Elisabeth Kübler-Ross' first research was interviewing patients who were confronting long- term illness and death.

There are also many kinds of illness that can result in damage to your body or leave you not as mobile as you once were. Cancer patients may lose a breast or undergo debilitating treatment. You may lose your eyesight or hearing or your ability to move easily. When you lose your health, you can lose your sense of yourself, and you may mourn that loss. You have to adapt to the new reality.

When a friend has been diagnosed with a life threatening illness, we can often feel helpless, not knowing how to help. When a loved one is diagnosed with Alzheimer's disease, we have essentially lost that person as we knew them. Caring for people with dementia or a disease such as ALS, will impact the spouse or relative over a long period of time. Knowing how to respond to a person who is ill is difficult. Even a chronic illness will change the dynamics of the family and we must be sensitive to those changes. Sometimes the individual or family may not want your help. Perhaps all you can do is to offer support to those who are the caregivers.

If we remember that grief is a universal experience and is not confined to the loss of a spouse, parent, or child, but reaches out into all levels of relationships and friendships, and beyond, we may be able to give comfort with the same gentle understanding that we would give our closest family or friends. We must never demean anyone's loss or grief, because we can never fully understand how deep their pain is. You must also remember that nobody else can fully understand *your* loss or pain.

Your decision: Will you look clearly at your loss and begin to understand how this loss has affected you and your family?

Questions:

1. Have you had losses other than your current loss? What were they?

2. Do these losses help you understand the grief of others?

3. Have there been conflicts or changes in your family relationships because of your loss?

Describe them.

4. If there are conflicts within your family, do you feel that it is possible to restore or improve your family relationships?

5. What do you think that you could do to resolve these problems?

Personal prayer:
Ask God to give you the faith to trust him as you move through this painful time.

HOW TO RECOVER FROM LOSS

And we know that in all things God works for the good of those who love him,
who have been called according to his purpose. Romans 8: 28

Chapter 6. Recovering

What is recovery?

I believe that the goal of recovery for the bereaved is to remember the past without the pain. To move into the future confident that God has a plan for your life and you are willing to live out that plan. It is to be free of the crippling pain that can thwart and stunt your life. If you have lost your health, the goal would be to accept your condition without bitterness or anger. This is a tough situation, since the future may not be better for you. But if you are to live with a chronic or increasingly debilitating illness, you have to go through the same process of grieving and recovery if you want to live an emotionally productive life.

If you have sustained the loss of a loved one, it is possible to recover from your grief. When the recovery is successful, you can start to look again towards the future. Before, there was no future, only the fact of the loss. With recovery you will be able to see that you will survive each day. Because you have made the choice to recover, you will be willing to move into a new phase with new challenges.

You can:
1. Recognize that you have survived
2. Make an assessment of where you are
3. See your life as a continuing process
4. Choose to live, not remain in the past
5. Decide not to be a victim, but choose to be happy
6. Acknowledge that you are responsible for your own happiness
7. Take responsibility for your future
8. Start to rebuild your relationship with God if it has faltered

If you are starting to recover, you can:
1. Distinguish the difference between loneliness and solitude:
   Loneliness will make you sad. Solitude will give you strength.
2. Remember the past without pain
3. Acknowledge both the good and the bad in your relationship with the lost person
4. Shift your focus from what has happened in the past to the future

What does it mean to recover from the loss of a loved one? It means remembering the past without the searing pain, choosing to be happy, and to be willing to enter into life again. What does acceptance mean for some who is desperately ill? It means reaching a place of acceptance of the circumstances, no longer being bitter or angry, being willing to accept the support of those who love you, and seeing God's love for us through it all.

Choosing to recover

Beginning to recover from grief consists of several decisions:

1. First, there must be a decision to recover.

    Not everyone chooses to recover from grief. We all have seen people who have spent their lives mourning their loss. But you can make the decision to recover. No one else can make this decision for you and no one else can do your grief work. Unless you take responsibility for your own recovery, you will not recover. As Jesus asked the invalid at the pool called Bethesda, you must answer the question: "Do you want to be well?" Do you want to recover? Books, counselors, groups, and friends can help you in the grieving process. But only *you* can make the decision to work through the grieving process to healing. If someone you care about is grieving, you can encourage him or her to recover.

2. There must be a decision to fight, to deal with your circumstances rather than denying or hiding from them.

3. There must be a decision to abide in your faith and trust God and to know that he is in control of all things.

4. And, there must be a willingness to start making changes in your life. It is hard to let go of our lives as they were before, but you won't recover unless you adapt to your new life.

It is very important that you choose to recover. You will not recover unless you do.

How to start the recovery process

1. Find a group or partner (someone who has experienced a similar loss).

    It is imperative that you have support. It is very difficult to recover alone. Find a friend who will understand, or a group that provides a safe, loving, nonjudgmental environment.

2. Make a commitment to recover:

    Be committed to work through your grief to recovery
    Be committed to stay with your grief group until you have recovered
    Be honest about your feelings and take time to understand your emotions
    Be willing to seek pastoral or professional help, if needed

3. Be willing to recognize non-productive behavior:

    Using alcohol or medication to numb the pain
    Considering the decision not to continue living (thoughts of suicide)
    Overeating or not eating
    Sleeping too much or too little

4. Recognize feelings of regret or guilt

Almost immediately after the death of a loved one, you may start to think about things that you wish had been different, things that you should have done or said, lost opportunities. Grieving people often experience the "If only..." stage: "If only I had insisted that he go to the doctor sooner." "If only we had taken that vacation that she wanted."

Memories of past hurts or pain, as well as perceived lost opportunities, are often the basis for deep feelings of regret or guilt. If your loss is that of health, you may feel that you might have been responsible for your illness. These regrets can be as deep-seated as those dealing with the death of a loved one, and if not resolved, will impede your recovery.

5. Deal with your regrets

How do you deal with these feelings of regret and guilt? Where there is real guilt over genuine misdeeds or mistakes in the past, there is no shortcut but to acknowledge them and ask God's forgiveness. If you realize that you did the best that you could in the past, there is no need for any regret. Sometimes pastoral counseling or sharing your feelings with another person makes it easier. As long as you hold on to your regrets you cannot recover. You must be able to forgive yourself and others for the past.

How long will it take to recover?

The grieving process normally takes from one to two years, although some people are able to recover more quickly. Sometimes grieving can go on for many years, although this is usually the result of not initially dealing with the grief. Just as there is no correct way to grieve, there is no yardstick to measure progress, only the sense of relief and the easing of pain.

Why is the length of time to grieve so different for everyone? It can depend on:

1. Your personality and your way of responding to painful events:

Some people may be able to complete their grieving and move on more quickly than others. This does not mean that if you have difficulty in recovering that you are weaker than somebody else. You are just different.

2. Whether the loss was sudden or foreseen:

A death preceded by a long illness may seem to give additional time to prepare for the loss. However, a lengthy illness does not always prepare you for the loss, and the strain of caring for the loved one may leave you even more vulnerable to stress.

3. The amount of support given you by family and friends.

If you have the support of loving family members and friends, it will help your recovery. Don't hesitate to reach out to them and ask for their help.

4. Prior losses and whether or not they have been fully mourned:

> If there have been insufficiently mourned losses in the past, these prior emotions may be newly triggered by the current loss. For example, if your mother had died when you were young and you had never fully experienced or recovered from that grief, the occurrence of a new loss might bring up all the feelings that you had when your mother died. These feelings might come flooding up again and intensify your current grief.

5. Whether or not you have ambivalent feelings about the loss:

> If it is a spouse or parent who has died, sometimes there may have been unresolved problems in the relationship or you may even be glad that the long illness is over and that you are now free to get on with your life. These seemingly inappropriate feelings can cause even more pain. Feelings of relief are normal so don't feel guilty about them.

6. The social, economic, and personal circumstances in which the individuals must do their grieving, for example: financial problems or poor health. If you have a strong support system of family or church members, this will aid your recovery.

7. Our social conditioning:

> Men and women often respond to a loss in different ways. A woman may be more willing to share her grief with others, to reach out to people around her, and to talk more openly about the loss. Men are more inclined to keep their grief to themselves, work hard to avoid losing control in front of others, and refrain from asking for help or assistance.

Your decision: Will you make the decision to recover?

This is not easy. It means taking a realistic inventory of your feelings and taking the time to talk about them with another person, or sharing your feelings with a recovery group or group of close friends. It means taking time to understand yourself and your grief. It means making the commitment to recover.

Questions:

> 1. Are there past losses in your life that you didn't mourn properly? Make a list of them.

2. Do you have any regrets about a part of your relationship with your loved one?

3. Have you been able to forgive yourself for the past?

4. Have you made the decision to recover?

Personal prayer:
Ask God to help you start your recovery process and to begin healing your wounded heart.

Rejoice in the Lord always. I will say it again: Rejoice! Let your gentleness be evident to all. The Lord is near. Do not be anxious about anything, but in everything, by prayer and petition, with thanksgiving, present your requests to God. And the peace of God, which transcends all understanding, will guard your hearts and your minds in Christ Jesus.
Philippians 4: 4-7

Chapter 7. Letting Go of the Past

Past Losses

How you react to a serious loss often reflects how you have dealt with losses in your past. A helpful exercise is to think back to previous losses (family pets, your grandparents, other relatives). Try to remember how you reacted to those losses. It is likely that you continue to unconsciously react the same way each time you face a loss. If you can remember how you dealt with past losses, it may help you to understand some of the ways you have been coping with this current loss.

Sometimes you discover that there are losses for which you have not completely grieved. Were you able to grieve sufficiently in the past or is there still pain over a past loss? It is also possible that you had an incomplete relationship with your loved one at the time of death; that you were unable to say goodbye to him or her, or that there were some unresolved issues in your relationship.

If you were not able to complete your grieving in the past, it may be because you were not able to satisfactorily conclude the relationship or say goodbye. Perhaps it was because of things unsaid or incomplete between you. This can be called an emotionally incomplete relationship. In order to resolve such an emotionally incomplete loss, you must be able to forgive yourself or the other person, to say what is needed, and to let go. If you have not been able to complete your grieving for a loss in the past, you can still complete it now. You can do it alone. **If you are able to complete your emotional relationship, and let go of the past, it does not mean you'll have to forget your loved one**.

How to identify an incomplete farewell

The first step is to find out what seems incomplete. What do you wish you had said or hadn't said? Do you wish that things could have been different? Does thinking about that person make you cry? Have you not been able to let go of that person? Does their loss still cause you pain?

When you weren't able to say goodbye; completing an incomplete farewell

If you had a good relationship with your loved one and there was time to talk before death occurred, you may have been able to say goodbye to one another. The relationship has been completed and you can be at peace.

However, for many people, there may be some factors that can contribute to a feeling of emotional incompleteness:

> Your loved one died suddenly, without time to express feelings
> There were some unresolved problems in the relationship
> There were things you wish you had said, or hadn't said
> There were things you regret or would have done differently

How to forgive others and yourself

Be kind and compassionate to one another, forgiving each other, just as in Christ God forgave you. Ephesians 4:32

At the heart of completing your relationships is forgiveness. You need to forgive others for their actions. Whether these hurts were real or imagined, you need to face them and forgive them. Forgiving people does not mean endorsing their actions, but now is the time to forgive your loved ones and let go of your memories of painful events.

You must also be willing to forgive yourself. You must be willing to recognize your part in contributing to a painful relationship by not discussing issues or expressing your feelings. As God has forgiven your sins through Christ, you can forgive yourself through his love. This may be difficult and take some time, but it is important for your recovery. Recognize that you did the best you could. The same is true for your loved ones. They did the best they could, too.

Dealing with anger

You may be angry with the person who died. It is important to resolve that anger. Some reasons for anger:

> Feelings of abandonment ("Why did you leave me?")
> The untimeliness of the death ("You weren't supposed to die now.")
> Incomplete estate planning ("What am I going to do with the business?")
> Panic ("How can I live without you?")

The death of a family member can severely change the relationships within that family. If there was a long illness, there may have been stresses in dealing with the illness that resulted in resentments, misunderstandings, and bad feelings. Instead of the loss bringing the family together, it often builds walls between spouses, parents and children, or between brothers and sisters. It is not uncommon for there to be angry feelings, either expressed or unexpressed. If this anger is not resolved, it is difficult to recover. Even if it seems impossible to resolve this anger face to face, it can be addressed unilaterally; resolving your own feelings through prayer and self-expression can be a start to mending broken communications within the family.

Expressing your feelings

An important part of recovery is expressing significant emotional statements. You may not have been able or had the time to say, "I love you," "I am proud of you," "I don't want you to leave me," "I'm sorry about what happened," "I'm still angry with you." Whatever it was that you were unable to communicate in the past, you can communicate now. Make a list of all the things you wanted to say to your lost one. If you could have your loved one back for one last conversation, what would you say?

If you are angry with a family member, write it out in a letter. This is a private letter and it will never be sent. Don't hold back your feelings. Express the depths of your anger, your disappointments, and your resentments. Not only do you need to say goodbye to the lost one, you also need to make a new start with the living. When your family relationships are broken, you have not only lost your loved one, but you have lost your closeness with those who remain. What do you want to say to them?

Saying goodbye

One of the best ways to say goodbye is by writing a letter to your loved one. Using your list of things you weren't able to say, write a letter expressing what you need to say now. You may express sorrow, anger, bitterness, or love. You may feel pain, but it's okay to cry. Make sure you say everything that needs to be said. Be as complete as you can.

You may not be ready to say goodbye to your loved one by writing a letter at this time. If not, remember that you can always do so later.

When you have written your letter, you need to communicate it. Read your letter out loud. Many psychologists suggest reading it to an empty chair or a beloved stuffed animal. Pretend that your loved one is really there. It is most effective if you can read your letter to a close friend.

Trust that this will work. If you start crying, keep going. If you're the listener, don't interrupt. When you get to the end of the letter and say "I love you," then it's time to tell your loved one goodbye. Not goodbye to the loving memories, but goodbye to the pain, confusion, and anguish. You'll feel an enormous sense of relief. You can now say farewell to your loved one and begin to move on.

Your decision: Can you take the steps necessary to let go of the past and say goodbye to your loved one?

Questions:

1. Make a list of all the past losses in your life and how you reacted to them. If you still have a tearful attachment to a loss, you may not have fully grieved that loss. Now is the time to complete that relationship and say goodbye.

2. Make a list of all the things you wish you had said but didn't.

3. Make a list of all the things you regret about the past. Can you forgive yourself for them?

4. Are you ready to write your letter? If you are, then do so. It doesn't have to be perfect.

5. Did you write your letter? If you did not write a letter or share it with someone, do you think that you can do it later?

Personal prayer:
If you have regrets, confess your feelings to God and ask his forgiveness. Let his comforting Spirit flow through you and feel his forgiveness and peace. Let go of your regret and any guilt you may feel.

HOW TO RECOVER FROM LOSS

"Just as the Father has loved me, I have also loved you; abide in my love. If you keep my commandments, you will abide in my love; just as I have kept my Father's commandments, and abide in his love. These things I have spoken to you, that my joy may be in you, and that your joy may be made full." John 15: 9-11

Chapter 8. Turning the Corner

Now you can look back to see where you have been. You have passed through the first shock of loss, begun to understand how little prepared you were to deal with your grief, and survived the depression of the second crisis when reality came crashing in. You have made the decision to recover and have some knowledge of the process of grieving. You may have identified incomplete relationships and prior incomplete grieving of past losses. You have learned how to say farewell to your loved ones.

Now you can begin to be aware of how your life has changed. Not just that your loved one or your previous good health is gone, but the other changes in your life. You are learning to take care of yourself. You are more aware of your loneliness, but you need this time to be alone and come to terms with all that you have experienced. You have learned that although you will always miss your loved one, he or she will always be with you in your heart and memories.

You can now be aware that you are ready to:

> Recognize your grieving as a positive and healing period in your life
> Recognize avoidance behavior (being unduly busy, being dependent on drugs)
> Recognize your anger and choosing to let go of it
> Resolve any remaining medical questions about the death
> Learn to live without your loved one or with your changed health
> Realize that it is healthy to begin to move on

Looking from the past towards the future
From this point you can start to look towards the future. Before, there was no future. Now you are able to lift your head and see that you will survive each day. Because you have made the choice to recover, you are willing to move into a new phase with new challenges. This phase of the grieving process includes:

> Recognizing that you have survived the loss
> Being able to make an assessment of where you are
> Seeing your life as a continuing process
> Choosing to live, not to remain in the past
> Deciding not to be a victim, not to be powerless
> Acknowledging that you are responsible for your own happiness
> Starting to rebuild your relationship with God if it has faltered
> Taking responsibility for your future

What you need to do:
> Realize that you will always miss your loved one.
> Remember the past without pain.
> Acknowledge both the bad and the good in your relationship with the lost person.
> Release resentment and anger. Shift your focus from what has happened to the future.

How to help yourself:
Let the people around you know that you are committed to recovery and that you would appreciate their help and their support.

List the people to whom you can turn for support:

Your decision:
> To accept that you can say goodbye without forgetting the loved one
> To learn to live your life without your loved one
> To be willing to make the changes in your life that will enable you to grow

Questions:

> 1. Do a personal inventory:
>> Have you been able to let go of anger?

>> Are you still often depressed?

>> Are you afraid of the future? Why?

2. What positive decisions have you made about recovering?

3. Is anything preventing you from recovering?

4. What could you do to remove these obstacles?

Personal prayer:
Ask God to help you discover your true identity as his child.

HOW TO RECOVER FROM LOSS

The Lord is my strength and my song; he has become my salvation.
Psalm 118: 14

Chapter 9. Building a new life

At this point you may feel confusion. Some of the extreme pain may have passed; you no longer live every moment of the day in despair. There is hope that you will recover. But recover to what? Your old life is gone, never ever to return as before. The vast hole in your life that your loved one's death or your loss of health has caused is still there. How can you go on? What will life be like?

During this time of finding new directions you may experience:

> A growing realization that your life has changed in many ways
> A reluctance to make the necessary changes in your life
> A realization that you are responsible for your own happiness
> A feeling of continuing loneliness and loss
> A realization that you must look at the future and let go of the past

This is a time of reevaluating where you have been by looking at your past life, your loss, your grieving. It is also a time when you must choose to look ahead to what can be for you. You do have a choice: you can stay within the confines of your past, always in grief, always in pain, or you can have the courage to find a new life. It will not be like the past. In some ways it will never be as good, but it will be different. It is not disloyal to your loved ones to enjoy your new life. It is not disloyal to choose to be happy.

You will always carry your loved one with you, as you carry memories of all of those who have died. You cannot continue to live in fear of your own illness or death. You cannot give up. But it is important that you continue to complete your own life. The tapestry of your life has not yet been completed; you must pick up the threads and continue to weave.

What you find as you look at the future:

> New hopes and ambitions
> That you are still dealing with fear of the future
> Learning that you will have to take some risks
> Realizing that the old comforting support system is no longer the same
> Learning to manage the change in your life
> Realizing that the grief will recur at intervals
> Learning from the past and integrating it into your future life
> Incorporating the memories of your loved one into your life
> Letting go of your loved one without losing what he or she meant to you

---

Your focus as you integrate the past with the future:
To connect the threads of the past with the future.

Internalizing the lost person
What do we mean by internalizing the lost person? When you have just lost someone to death, there is a time when you feel very close physically to that person. Active grieving maintains that closeness, and there are sometimes fears that if you stop grieving you will lose that last bond. But slowly, as you let go of the grieving and begin to remember more objectively what you recall about that person, you bring what you remember into your inner self where you can carry your memories in your heart without pain. It means being able to remember and talk about your lost one with a loving fondness. The past is not lost, but has become part of you and your life. It means bringing together the past and the present so there is no longer a division. There is no longer a time before death or a time after. All of this is your life, and your lost one will always be part of that life.

Areas of special difficulty:
There can be problems in the family unit: When there is a death within the family, the dynamics of that family change and a new family system may need to be devised and new roles accepted. The remaining children must be given attention and not made to carry the burden of the lost sibling or parent. Family members all grieve differently; you must be sensitive to their grief.

Problems in the marriage after a loss of a child, parent, sibling, or health:
You may need to resolve issues of anger, guilt, remorse, or blame. The grieving process often alienates spouses rather than drawing them closer together. Especially if there is the loss of a child, the parents may blame themselves or each other for the circumstances of the loss.

If there has been significant loss of health or mobility of a family member, the whole family needs to adjust to that loss. Feelings of resentment, discouragement, and fear of future loss need to be recognized.

Families may need help in resolving these issues or conflicts. Professional counseling can be helpful in reestablishing healthy family relationships.

How to help yourself:
You need people around you who realize that you have issues to work through to reestablish yourself in life, but who also know you are capable of meeting and resolving these issues.

Your decision: You must choose to understand yourself, take action, and plan what you are going to do. You must choose to work through the conflicts in your life and the conflicts between the past and the future.

Questions:

1. As you work through your problems of adjustment to your loss, which are the most difficult for you? Place them in these categories:

Practical Problems: Possible Solutions:

Relational (People) Problems: Possible Solutions:

2. Are you willing to look for new solutions to problems? Where would you look?

3. Are there problems you think you can't do anything about?

4. Can you either resolve or accept the problems you can't do anything about?

Personal prayer:
Share your fears of the future with God and ask him for courage and peace.

HOW TO RECOVER FROM LOSS

"For I know the plans I have for you," declares the Lord, "plans to prosper you and not to harm you, plans to give you a hope and a future. Then you will call upon me and come and pray to me, and I will listen to you. You will seek me and find me when you seek me with all your heart." Jeremiah 29: 11-13

Chapter 10. Summing Up

It is impossible to know how long the grieving period will last for you. It may take ten months or longer, but two years is about average. But it is also important to know that recovery is possible. It is possible to once again have fun, laugh, do exciting things, and be happy. This process of grieving and recovery takes time. It cannot be rushed through. The more thoughtfully you proceed, the better the results will be. Your task now is to begin to integrate your grief experiences into your whole life and look to the future.

Moving on beyond loss

When your loved one died, his or her life came to an end. When you lost your former good health, your life changed forever. You are now a survivor and you have a life to complete. In the woven tapestry of your life, one strand ended, another continues. Life as you knew it may not exist anymore, but you have been given the chance for a new life. What you make of it is up to you. If this sounds like another choice, it is. You can choose to remain static, not moving forward, or you can move on with your life.

What you do with the rest of your life depends upon how actively you seek new goals and new purpose for your life. It takes a lot of time to recover from traumatic grief. Don't be impatient. Take your time. When the time comes to "pick up your mat and walk," you will know that you are ready. Don't be surprised if the sadness revisits you from time to time; chances are, it always will. There may be more tears at the most unlikely and inconvenient times, but knowing that your grieving has been necessary and cleansing, you can be confident that a new life awaits you.

There are some positive feelings:

    Joy in living and choosing to be happy
    Return to a steady state of balance
    Increased capacity to appreciate people and things
    More tolerance and understanding of others' grief
    Desire to find new friendships and relationships
    A sense of play and freedom
    A deepening of your faith

Some new life experiences:

    Finding deeper resources of strength
    Choosing to fully participate in life
    Accepting that life will always be full of change

Accepting your own mortality
Seeking a purpose for your life
Having a more positive view of life
Finding contentment through God's love

In conclusion:
If you have read this far and have started, even tentatively, your plan to recover, you have accomplished much. You have:

Acknowledged that you are in pain
Faced your loss
Understood why the world views you as it does
Recognized that the grief returns again and again
Remembered your past losses
Forgiven yourself and your loved ones
Looked for the first time at the future
Decided to let change happen in your life

You are beginning to:

Understand the grieving process
Let go of your loved ones and your former life
Say goodbye in the midst of your remembering
Discover new roles
Integrate your past with your future
Feel back in balance
Move beyond loss

God's invitation to a new life:
As God's word to us in Deuteronomy 30:19 commanded, *"Now choose life, so that you and your children may live and that you may love the Lord your God, listen to his voice, and hold fast to him."* God is not finished with you. He is writing the next chapter of your life. You must have courage, overcome your fear, be fully alive, and live with hope. Your hope is that life can become better for you as you live with God's power in your life. It is a question of hope versus despair. Which will you choose?

Recovering from the death of a loved one is one of the most difficult things you will ever have to face, and is physically, emotionally, and spiritually exhausting. Recovering from a traumatic illness or facing future illness is equally distressing. You have every reason to feel lost. But with the help of God and the support of others who understand your pain you do have hope and know that you will recover. You can have the confidence to continue to work through the grieving process and will not only survive, but also fully live again.

Questions:

1. Where do you think you are now in your grieving process? (Place a mark on the line)

_____

Date of loss

Recovery

2. How can you move forward across this line?

3. Are you able to see a new horizon of recovery and renewed joy in life?

4. Do you believe you can now begin to draw on what you have learned to comfort others and to help others to understand their loss?

Personal prayer:
Thank God for his support in guiding you through your grieving process and ask him to help you move ahead toward wholeness.

HOW TO RECOVER FROM LOSS

Frequently Asked Questions:

1. It is appropriate to keep photos of the deceased person on view?

Why not? Your loved one was a central part of your life and you want to remember him or her. If it gives you pleasure to have photos around the house, then do so. Don't feel that you have to explain to visitors; it's not a symptom of abnormality. If relatives feel uncomfortable about photos, remind them that it is your house and you are able to make your own decisions.

2. How often should I go to the cemetery to visit the burial site?

Whenever it seems natural for you to do so. As time passes, you may find that the number of visits lessens. There are no rules about this and you don't need to explain to anyone.

3. What about the anniversary of the death?

Most people mark the date by visiting the burial site either with friends and family or alone. You should prepare for the date and plan to be with someone who understands if that would be helpful. It's OK to be sad and relive the events of the death and funeral. Part of the grieving process is letting yourself feel your grief. Don't be surprised if you are somewhat depressed at this time of year. This will get better with time.

4. When should I remove my loved one's clothing and personal belongs from the house?

There is no time limit on this. Some people feel better giving the clothing away soon after death; others wait a year or more. If you wait a long period of time, it does not necessarily mean that you are not recovering, only that you are not yet ready to undertake the task. Sometimes asking a friend or relative to help you may make it easier. As you get older, you may have more losses and more personal effects to distribute. It should get easier, but often it's not. Removing furnishings and clothing from a parent's home is especially difficult. Ask someone to help you do this.

5. What should I keep of my loved one's personal effects?

Whatever you want. Keep those things that are meaningful to you. It is not always healthy to keep a room exactly as your loved one left it. You may need some professional counseling to make decisions about this.

6. When should I take off my wedding rings?

There is no specific time period of mourning in our society, so it is up to you. Some people are comfortable with their rings and continue to wear them indefinitely; others wear them until a time when it seems appropriate to remove them. If removing your rings makes you feel uncomfortable, don't do it. You'll know when you are ready.

---

7. If I have lost a spouse, should I consider marrying again?
If you have recovered and feel like a whole person again and find someone who also is a whole person whom you can love and live with, it's a wonderful idea. It is not disloyal to your departed spouse. A new marriage can bring great joy to your life

HOW TO RECOVER FROM LOSS

How to Survive the Holidays

There are really only two ways to deal with special days and holidays: flee them or face them. There is nothing wrong with leaving town and doing something entirely different. It is equally OK to stay and see it through, even though there may be some pain involved. However, it is hard to escape the prologue to the holidays. Easter seems to start in January, the Fourth of July looms large all summer, plans for Thanksgiving get under way in September, and Christmas starts in October! So the pressure mounts. You have to make decisions about where you will be, what you will do, whom you will see. This can be very painful as you seek to reconcile the past with the present. It is important that you learn to deal with holidays, as they are a yearly occurrence, and each year you must face them anew.

There are choices you can make to help you through the tough times. It is not necessary to be miserable and in fact you may find new ways to enjoy the holiday times. Here are some suggestions for you as the holidays approach:

1. Recognize that the holidays may be difficult for you as memories come sweeping back. Don't let them creep up on you. Be prepared.

2. Realize that there will be some pain and depression and that there are no magical solutions. Plan your days ahead of time so that you aren't too stressed or too lonely.

3. Don't try to do too much. You don't have to prove anything to yourself or anyone. Give yourself time to rest and be with people you love.

4. Don't be afraid to make changes. Now is the time to let go of old traditions and start some new ones. On the other hand, if doing things the same way is more comfortable, do it.

5. Let your family and friends know about your feelings. Don't just go along with their plans. Get together early in the season to decide what you are going to do and then stick with it.

6. Let others take more of the responsibility for gatherings and food. You don't have to provide everything for everybody. Don't feel guilty and learn to say no.

7. Do your shopping early. If you don't feel like exchanging gifts, you may want to eliminate it this year. Be flexible.

8. Don't neglect your health. Eat sensibly and get regular exercise other than shopping.

9. Be sure you have some plans for special holiday events: Easter Services, Thanksgiving Dinner, Christmas Eve, or New Year's Eve. Don't be alone. Invite some friends to be with you for dinner. Attending a church service with friends may help start your new year with hope.

10. Center your activities and thoughts more on the real meaning of Christmas. Let God comfort you during his own special time of year.

How to Survive the Holidays

What to do about:

Christmas Cards
> If you decide to send cards, start writing them early.
> You can choose not to send cards this year; your friends will understand.
> Writing a letter instead of sending cards might feel more appropriate.

Christmas Music
> Be prepared to hear carols when you are shopping or in public places.
> Use your own tapes in the car and at home.
> Choose some new music to listen to and enjoy.

Shopping and Gift Giving
> If you decide to give gifts, shop early to avoid stress.
> Remember that you have the option to not give gifts this year.
> Give only those gifts that you want to give: give from the heart.
> Don't give in to the pressure that you have to do more than you are able to do.

Holiday Decorating and Tree Trimming
> Do only what you feel like doing. This is not Homes and Gardens time.
> You may want to have the same size tree and decorate as usual. That's OK.
> If you have a tree, invite friends to help you decorate.
> Remember you have the option not to have a tree or to do something different.
> If you will be away during the holidays don't bother with decorating.

Cooking
> If baking and cooking gives you pleasure, do it!
> If spending time in the kitchen is painful, forget it!

In all these matters, remember that you have the option to:
> 1. Keep the old traditions
> 2. Change the traditions
> 3. Do whatever you want
> 4. Do nothing at all!

Remember, it's your decision!

HOW TO RECOVER FROM LOSS

Scripture

"Blessed are those who mourn, for they will be comforted." Matthew 5: 4

*Even though I walk through the valley of the shadow of death, I will fear no evil;
for you are with me; your rod and your staff, they comfort me. Psalm 23: 4*

*The Lord is close to the broken hearted
and saves those who are crushed in spirit. Psalm 34: 18*

*Turn to me and be gracious to me, for I am lonely and afflicted.
The troubles of my heart have multiplied; free me from my anguish.
Look upon my affliction and my distress and take away all my sins. Psalm 25: 16-18*

*"And surely, I am with you always, to the end of the age." Matthew 28: 20.
"As I was with Moses, so I will be with you; I will never leave you nor forsake you."
Joshua 1: 5*

*And we know that in all things God works for the good of those who love him,
who have been called according to his purpose. Romans 8: 28*

*Rejoice in the Lord always. I will say it again: Rejoice! Let your gentleness be evident to
all. The Lord is near. Do not be anxious about anything, but in everything, by prayer and
petition, with thanksgiving, present your requests to God. And the peace of God, which
transcends all understanding, will guard your hearts and your minds in Christ Jesus.
Philippians 4: 4-7*

*"Just as the Father has loved me, I have also loved you; abide in my love.
If you keep my commandments, you will abide in my love;
just as I have kept my Father's commandments, and abide in his love.
These things I have spoken to you, that my joy may be in you,
and that your joy may be made full." John 15: 9-11*

*The Lord is my strength and my song; he has become my salvation.
Psalm 118: 14*

*"For I know the plans I have for you," declares the Lord, "plans to prosper you
and not to harm you, plans to give you a hope and a future.
Then you will call upon me and come and pray to me, and I will listen to you.
You will seek me and find me when you seek me with all your heart."
Jeremiah 29: 11-13*

Scripture

"For my thoughts are not your thoughts, neither are your ways my ways,"
declares the Lord.
"As the heavens are higher than the earth, so are my ways higher than your ways
and my thoughts than your thoughts." Isaiah 55: 8-9

Then Job replied to the Lord:
"I know that you can do all things; no plan of yours can be thwarted.
You asked 'Who is this that obscures my counsel without knowledge?'
Surely I spoke of things I did not understand,
things too wonderful for me to know." Job 42: 1-3

"I am the vine; you are the branches. If a man abides in me and I in him,
he will bear much fruit; apart from me you can do nothing." John 15: 5

Praise be to the God and Father of our Lord Jesus Christ,
the Father of compassion and the God of all comfort;
who comforts us in all our troubles, so that we can comfort
those in any trouble with the comfort we ourselves have received from God.
2 Corinthians 1: 3

"Here I am! I stand at the door and knock. If anyone hears my voice and opens the door,
I will come in and will dine with him, and he with me." Revelation 3: 20

"I am the resurrection and the life.
He who believes in me will live, even though he dies;
and whoever lives and believes in me will never die." John 11: 25

"Now choose life so that you and your children may live and that you may love the Lord
your God, listen to his voice, and hold fast to him. For the Lord is your life, and he will
give you many years in the land he swore to give to your fathers,
Abraham, Isaac and Jacob." Deuteronomy 30: 19

HOW TO RECOVER FROM LOSS

Bibliography and Selected Reading

Bibliography

Seven Choices. Elizabeth Harper Neeld, PhD. Warner Books, Inc. 1271 Avenue of the Americas, New York, 1990, 2003. A personally applied approach to the grieving process based on the premise that we must make choices in order to recover.

The Grief Recovery Handbook. John W. James and Frank Cherry. Harper and Row, 1988 Practical emphasis on processing grief and dealing with past losses through the study of a personal Loss History Graph.

On Death and Dying. Elisabeth Kübler-Ross. Macmillan, New York, 1969 The research of Kübler-Ross is the basis of much of what we know about the grieving process, both before and after the death of a loved one.

Silent Grief: Living in the Wake of Suicide. Christopher Lukas and Henry M. Seiden, PhD. Charles Scribner's Sons. 866 Third Avenue, New York, 10022. An extremely helpful book for those who have lost someone to suicide.

Beyond Grief: A Guide for Recovering from the Death of a Loved One. Carol Staudacher. New Harbinger Publications, Inc. Oakland, California. 1987

The NIV Study Bible, New International Version. Zondervan Bible Publishers. Grand Rapids, Michigan. 1985

Other helpful books:

The Courage to Grieve. Judy Tatlebaum. Lippincott & Crowell, 1980 Good, positive self-help book offering specific techniques for grief work and resolution.

A Grief Observed. C. S. Lewis. Bantam, NY, 1961

Grief Work. Velma D. Stevens. Broadman Press, Nashville, Tennessee, 1990

52 Simple Ways to Make Christmas Special. Jan Dargatz, Oliver Nelson Books, Publishers. 1991

ABOUT THE AUTHOR

Robyn Ledwith Mar is a graduate of Stanford University and a breast cancer survivor. She is the mother of four adult children and has six grandchildren. She was widowed at age 56 and was asked by her pastor to start a support group for other widows and widowers in the church. Based on her own grief and loss experience and research into the grieving process, she wrote *Grief Recovery, A Workbook for Widows and Widowers*, followed by *How to Recover from Loss, Understanding and Recovering from Grief* for general loss. Robyn has been leading groups and counseling the bereaved for over 20 years. She has remarried and lives in Los Altos Hills, California.

Also by
Robyn Ledwith Mar

Grief Recovery
A Workbook for Widows and Widowers
AuthorHouse 2010
www.authorhouse.com

HOW TO RECOVER FROM LOSS

Notes and Journaling

HOW TO RECOVER FROM LOSS

Notes and Journaling

HOW TO RECOVER FROM LOSS

Notes and Journaling

HOW TO RECOVER FROM LOSS

Notes and Journaling

HOW TO RECOVER FROM LOSS

Notes and Journaling

HOW TO RECOVER FROM LOSS

Notes and Journaling

Made in the USA
Charleston, SC
26 October 2012